Sorting

David Kirkby

RIGBY
INTERACTIVE LIBRARY

© 1996 Rigby Education
Published by Rigby Interactive Library,
an imprint of Rigby Education,
division of Reed Elsevier, Inc.
500 Coventry Lane,
Crystal Lake, IL 60014

Cover designed by Herman Adler Design Group.
Designed by The Pinpoint Design Company
Printed in China

00 99 98 97 96
10 9 8 7 6 5 4 3 2 1

Library of Congress Cataloging-in-Publication Data
Kirkby, David, 1943–
    Sorting / David Kirkby.
        p.   cm. — (Mini math)
    Summary: Presents simple activities to demonstrate
the concept of sorting, using categories like color,
shape, and function.
    ISBN 1-57572-006-X
    1. Set theory—Juvenile literature.   [1. Set theory.]
I. Title.   II. Series: Kirkby, David, 1943– Mini math.
QA248.K433   1996
511.3'22—dc20   95-38708
                                                   CIP
                                                   AC

Acknowledgments
The publishers would like to thank the following for the
kind loan of equipment and materials used in this book:
Boswells, Oxford; The Early Learning Centre; Lewis',
Oxford; W.H. Smith; N.E.S. Arnold. Special thanks to the
children of St Francis C.E. First School.

Photography: Chris Honeywell, Oxford

Contents

This is a block graph.

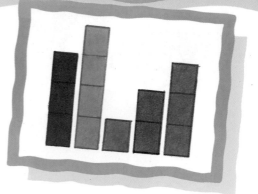

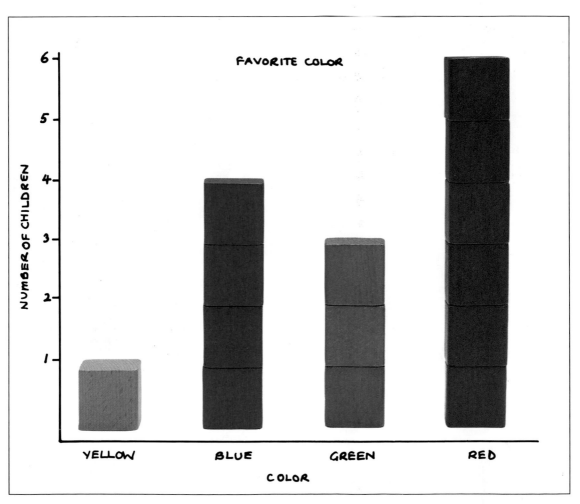

FAVORITE COLOR

NUMBER OF CHILDREN

YELLOW BLUE GREEN RED

COLOR

Count the blocks for each color. This block graph shows us that red is the most popular color.

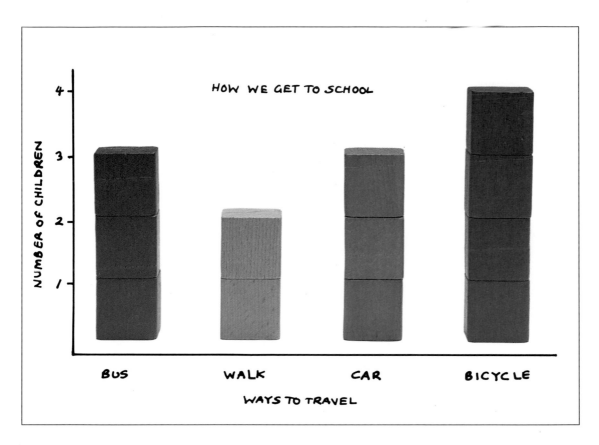

HOW WE GET TO SCHOOL

NUMBER OF CHILDREN

4

3

2

1

BUS   WALK   CAR   BICYCLE

WAYS TO TRAVEL

How many children travel by bus?
What else does the block graph
show you?

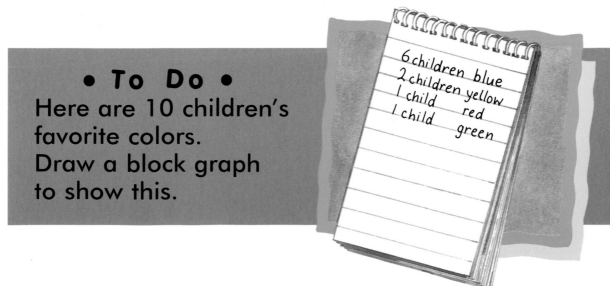

• To Do •
Here are 10 children's
favorite colors.
Draw a block graph
to show this.

6 children blue
2 children yellow
1 child   red
1 child   green

SPRING	
SUMMER	
AUTUMN	
WINTER	

This is a pictograph. It uses pictures or drawings.

BOYS

GIRLS

This pictograph shows how many boys and girls there are on our team.

On which days did I eat exactly
2 slices of bread?

MONDAY	
TUESDAY	
WEDNESDAY	
THURSDAY	
FRIDAY	
SATURDAY	
SUNDAY	

What else does the pictograph
tell you?

• To Do •
Draw a pictograph to
show how many apples
you eat this week.

Tallies are used to keep count.
They are grouped in fives.

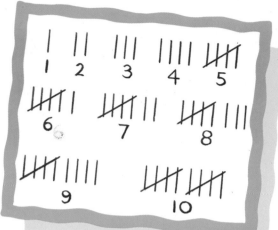

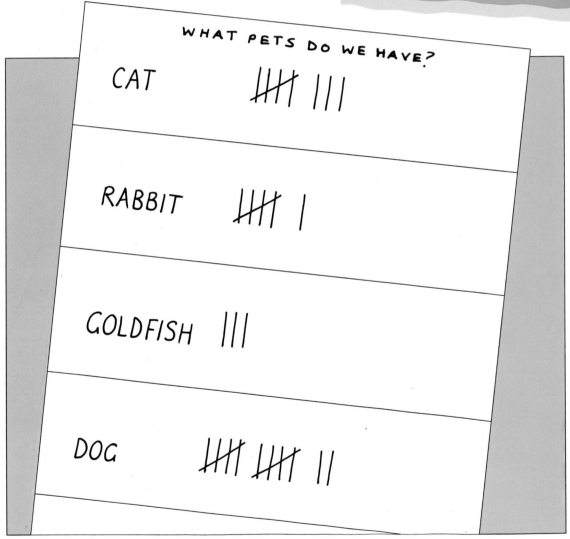

A dog is the most common pet.

Are the tallies correct?

• To Do •

Throw a number cube 10 times. Draw a tally chart to show the results.

This is a bar graph.
These are the bars.

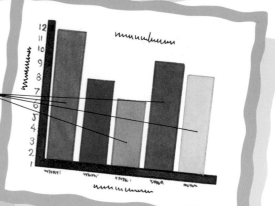

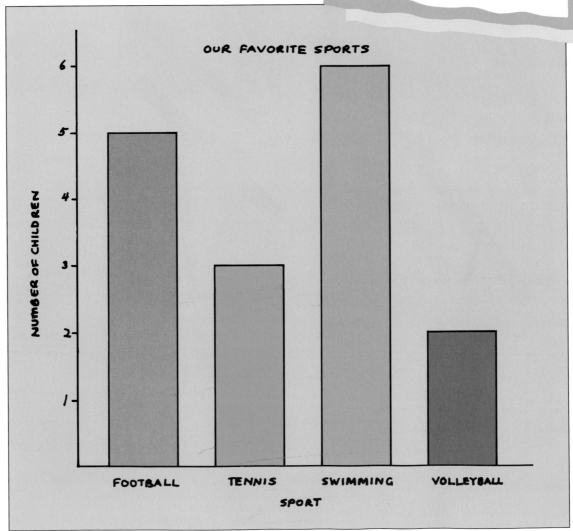

Swimming is the favorite sport,
then football.

How many children have green eyes?

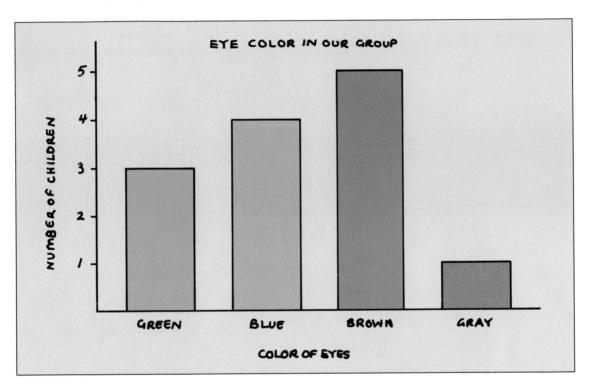

EYE COLOR IN OUR GROUP

NUMBER OF CHILDREN

COLOR OF EYES

GREEN   BLUE   BROWN   GRAY

What else does this bar graph show you?

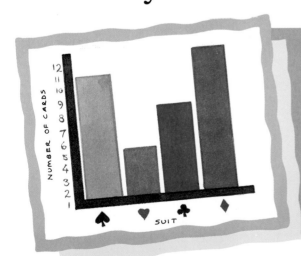

NUMBER OF CARDS

SUIT

• To Do •

Deal out 20 cards. Draw a bar graph to show how many cards of each suit there are.

A list helps you to remember things.

Gym Bag

shorts
T-shirt
gym shoes
socks

6 eggs
potatoes
bag of sugar
toothpaste
soap

This is a shopping list.

Some things on this menu are in the wrong place.

MENU

Drinks
Milk Shakes
Tea
Orange juice
Roast chicken

Main Course
Ice cream
Fish
Pasta
Burger and fries

Dessert
Apple pie
Pizza
Chocolate cake

Can you put them in
the right place?

Today's Jobs

● To Do ●
Make a list of things
you need to do today.

In some card games, you need to sort the cards.

These cards have been sorted into sets.

How have these cards been sorted?

• To Do •

Find a pack of
cards.
Find different ways
of sorting them.

A Venn diagram uses circles to sort things.

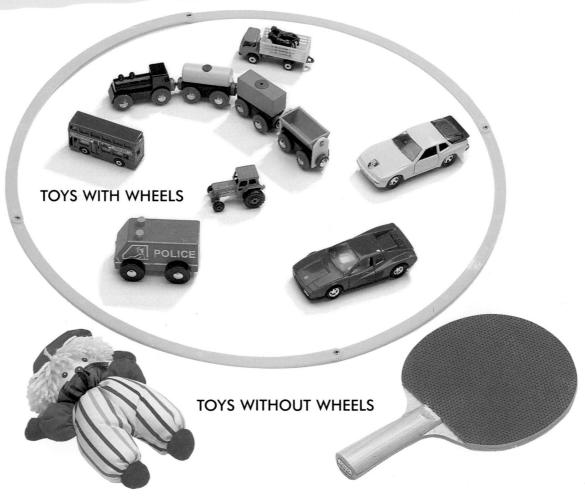

TOYS WITH WHEELS

TOYS WITHOUT WHEELS

These objects have been sorted inside and outside the circle.

18

STRAIGHT SIDES

CURVED SIDES

Where should the children put their shapes?

numbers more than 3

numbers less than 6

1 2 3 4 5 6 7 8 9 10

• To Do •
Where do these numbers go on this Venn diagram?

Sometimes we have to work out how things have been sorted.

Katy and Kieran have sorted the cookies.

How has the bread been sorted?

• To Do •

Here are 8 things you can eat.
Sort them into groups.

A survey helps us find things out.

Do you like Pizza?
☐ YES
☐ NO

What is your favorite fruit?

In some surveys we vote.
Voting means choosing.

In some surveys we answer questions.
How many children have been surveyed here?

• To Do •
Do your own survey. Find out some friends' favorite drinks.

Page 5	Jump rope **To Do:** Chocolate
Page 7	3 children travel by bus. 2 children walk. 3 children travel by car. 4 children travel by bicycle.
Page 9	2 slices on Tuesday and Sunday 4 slices on Monday 1 slice on Wednesday and Saturday 5 slices on Thursday 3 slices on Friday
Page 11	Yes, the tallies are correct.
Page 13	3 children have green eyes. 4 children have blue eyes. 5 children have brown eyes. 1 child has gray eyes.
Page 15	Roast chicken is a main course. Ice cream is a dessert. Pizza is a main course.
Page 17	Red cards, sixes, picture cards, numbers in order
Page 19	Red square goes in the blue circle. Blue half-circle goes in the middle (in both circles). **To Do:** 6, 7, 8, 9, and 10 go in the top. 4 and 5 go in the middle. 1, 2, and 3 go in the bottom.
Page 21	The bread is sorted into loaves and rolls.
Page 23	10 children